TAKING THE FIRST STEP TO FINANCIAL SECURITY

A PRIMER ON FINANCIAL LITERCY

BY

KEN MOLLAN

COPYRIGHT

ISBN:

978-1962224871 (Paperback)
978-1962224888 (Hardback)

TABLE OF CONTENTS

DEDICATION

This book is dedicated to my loving wife, Linda, and my two daughters, Melissa and Jessica. If not for their love and support, I would not be the man that I am. It is their love and support where my true wealth lies.

ABOUT THE AUTHOR

Kenneth A. Mollan (Ken) has taken a non-linear career path, which has led him to a diversified life experience. After graduating from Northern Illinois University DeKalb, IL, with a degree in Marketing/Finance, he went to work for the Hartford Insurance Company as an all-lines investigative insurance adjuster. There, he handled claims ranging from property losses, medical malpractice, auto, surety-bond, and worker's comp to general liability.

He left that position to be the claims manager for a former legacy trucking company; that opportunity led to a 25-year career in transportation logistics. However, while working in the logistics industry, he obtained his series 6 and 63 Licenses and later went on to obtain his life and health license and his property and casualty license.

In 1995, he was the co-founder and President of Ear-Clear, Inc., a manufacturer of the Sta-Put pet station, a pet feeding system. The introduction into the marketplace was on QVC, and since then, the Sta-Put Pet station has sold worldwide through being carried by Sharper Image, Orvis, Hammacher-Schlemmer, Sky Mall and others. The product currently has been licensed to Flipo Group and is again available through QVC and Amazon. Ken is an inventor and holder of two patents.

In the spring of 2000, he founded Seventh Wave Investments, a real estate and asset portfolio company; this is a privately held equity group.

In January 2004, Ken obtained his real estate license, and in October of 2005 obtained his Real Estate Appraiser License, and in November 2006, he became a Certified Residential Appraiser; after working for another appraisal firm for several years, Ken opened up his own appraisal firm, Greater Midwest Appraisals, LLC in 2013, which he currently operates with a staff of five appraisers, they perform both residential, commercial appraisals and consultations. Ken is a Certified Residential Appraiser in both Illinois and Colorado.

In January 2008, Ken founded First Step Financial Educators, the precursor to this book. Ken is a serial entrepreneur, having founded several companies, including Peddle Power Promotions, an eco-friendly bicycle-powered advertising and promotions company. BEYOND Home Performance, a company that performed an audit on a person's home sustainability and energy efficiency. He founded Starved Rock Pedi-Cab and Steamboat Basin Livery.

Both these companies operate as interpretive eco-tours along the Illinois–Michigan Canal in North Central Illinois. The tours detail the importance of the Illinois-Michigan Canal, and how the canal served as a linchpin for world trade from New Orleans to the eastern seaboard. There have been several more businesses that were less successful but provided invaluable learning experiences.

Ken is married and lives with his wife Linda and their 3-pound Yorkie named Sophie. Ken and Linda have two daughters, Melissa and Jessica; both are successful in their own right. Ken enjoys traveling, especially to Maui, kayaking, hiking, and camping. He writes a travel blog, called TRAVELKEN.com; he is currently teaching himself how to play the ukulele.

Ken has written this book out of necessity; what is in this book is not being taught in our schools, leaving generations ill-equipped with the tools and skill sets that can help ensure financial security and independence.

FOREWORD

In a world where financial uncertainties can often feel like an impenetrable maze, the path to trust and security begins with knowledge. "Taking Your First Step to Financial Security: A Primer on Financial Literacy" is more than just a book; it's your guide to navigating the complex landscape of personal finance with confidence and clarity.

This primer is crafted to provide you with easy-to-understand essential insights into key as of financial planning, ensuring you have a strong foundation to build upon as you work towards achieving your monetary goals.

It's time to take that first step—let this book be your trusted companion on the road to financial empowerment.

MANAGING YOUR CHECKBOOK REGISTER

Filling out a check register is a simple yet important task to keep track of your financial transactions, particularly when writing checks or making electronic payments. A check register is a record-keeping tool that helps you monitor your account balance, track expenses, and avoid overdrafts. Here's how to fill out a check register

The checkbook register is usually at the back of your checkbook. Record the starting Balance. Write the balance at the top of the first page.

Locate your current balance before you enter any new transaction.

Enter the new transaction.

DATE: Write the date of the transaction.

CHECK NUMBER: Include the check number, and keep it in sequential order.

DESCRIPTION: Describe who and why for the transaction.

DEPOSIT: If the transaction involves a deposit or adds to your balance, enter that amount in that column.

BALANCE: Calculate and update the balance after each transaction. For the first transaction, subtract the payment amount from the starting balance.

For subsequent transactions, add or subtract the transaction amount from the previous balance. For subsequent transactions, add or subtract the transaction amount from the previous balance.

REMEMBER to include all transactions, even those that don't involve checks, such as direct deposit payroll or automatic bill pay.

RECONCILE YOUR BALANCE: Periodically, reconcile your check register with your bank statement to ensure your recorded transactions match the bank's statement.

RECORD ALL CHARGES OR CREDITS THAT AFFECT YOUR ACCOUNT

DATE	CHECK NUMBER	DESCRIPTION	PAYMENT	C ✓	DEPOSIT	BALANCE $	
MEMO LINE:			EXPENSE CODE:				
MEMO LINE:			EXPENSE CODE:				
MEMO LINE:			EXPENSE CODE:				
MEMO LINE:			EXPENSE CODE:				
MEMO LINE:			EXPENSE CODE:				
MEMO LINE:			EXPENSE CODE:				
MEMO LINE:			EXPENSE CODE				
MEMO LINE:			EXPENSE CODE				
MEMO LINE:			EXPENSE CODE:				
MEMO LINE:			EXPENSE CODE:				
MEMO LINE:			EXPENSE CODE:				
MEMO LINE:			EXPENSE CODE:				
MEMO LINE:			EXPENSE CODE:				

REMEMBER TO RECORD AUTOMATIC PAYMENTS / DEPOSITS ON DATE AUTHORIZED.

CREDIT CARDS VS. DEBIT CARDS

Credit Cards: A credit card is a financial tool that allows you to borrow money from a bank or credit card company to make purchases. Here's how it works:

Borrowed Money: When you use a credit card to buy something, you're essentially borrowing money from the credit card issuer to complete the purchase.

Credit Limit: Each credit card has a predetermined credit limit, which is the maximum amount of money you can borrow using the card. Your credit limit is set by the issuer based on your creditworthiness. This is where your FICO SCORE is used to help determine your creditworthiness.

Monthly Payments: At the end of each billing cycle (usually a month), the credit card company sends you a statement that lists all your transactions during that period.

Minimum Payment: You're required to make at least a minimum payment on your outstanding balance each month. This is usually a small percentage of your total balance, but you can choose to pay more.

Interest Charge: If you don't pay your full balance by the due date, the remaining balance carries over to the next month and incurs interest charges. Interest rates on credit cards can be relatively high. Currently, credit card interest rates run from 20.68% to 22.74%; I refer you to the chapter on Rule 72 and how understanding Rule 72 works when borrowing money and the interest being paid.

Revolving Credit: Credit cards offer revolving credit, meaning you can continue to use the card as long as you stay within your credit limit and make at least the minimum payment on time. Your retail store cards, such as Kohl's, JC Penney, and Macy's, are revolving credit cards.

Debit Cards: A debit card, on the other hand, is directly linked to your bank account and allows you to spend the money you already have in your account. Here's how it works:

Linked to a Bank Account: A debit card is usually issued by your bank and is directly linked to your checking or savings account.

No borrowing: Unlike credit cards, you are not borrowing money when you use a debit card. You're simply accessing the funds you already have.

No Interest Charges: Since you're not borrowing money, there is no interest charges associated with debit card transactions.

No Monthly Statements: There are no monthly bills or invoices like with credit cards, as you're using your own money. You will see your transactions on your checking account statements.

Overdraft Protection: Some banks offer overdraft protection, which allows you to make purchases even if you don't have enough funds in your account. However, this may incur an overdraft. Cautionary tale; make sure all debit card transactions get recorded in the checking account register to prevent being overdrawn and incurring an overdraft charge.

SUMMARY

In conclusion, credit cards allow you to borrow money and pay it back later, often with interest, while debit cards enable you to spend your own money directly from your bank account. Each has its advantages and considerations, and your choice between them depends on your financial goals and spending habits. In my upcoming book, taking *The Next Step: Walking Towards Wealth*, we will deal with how to use credit or other people's money to your financial advantage.

RULE OF 72:

The "Rule of 72" is a simple mathematical formula used to estimate the approximate time it takes for an investment to double in value based on a fixed annual interest rate. To use the Rule, you divide 72 by the annual interest rate (expressed as a percentage). The result is an estimate of the number of years it will take for your initial investment to double.

Formula: Years to Double = 72 / Annual Interest rate (%)

For example, if you have an investment with an annual interest rate of 8%, according to the Rule of 72, it would take approximately 9 years for that investment to double in value (72 / 8 = 9).

Compounding Interest: Compound interest is the process of earning interest not only on the initial amount of money you invest (or deposit) but also on the accumulated interest over time. In other words, you're earning interest on your interest. This can lead to significant growth of your money over time.

Here's how it works: When interest is compounded, the interest earned in each compounding period (which could be annually, quarterly, monthly, etc.) is added to the principal amount. In the next compounding period, interest is calculated on the new total, including the previously earned interest. This cycle continues, and over time, the compounding effect causes your investment to grow faster than simple interest, where interest is only earned on the initial principal.

In essence, compounding interest allows your money to work for you more effectively, leading to exponential growth in the long run. It's a fundamental concept in finance and investing that helps individuals and businesses accumulate wealth over time.

NET WORTH

Net worth is a financial term that represents the difference between a person's or entity's total assets and their total liabilities. In simple terms, net worth is a measure of an individual's or organization's financial health and wealth. It provides insight into how much value is left over after all debts and obligations have been subtracted from the total value of their assets.

Here's how you can calculate net worth:

NET WORTH = TOTAL ASSETS – TOTAL LIABILITIES

Total Assets: This includes all the valuable possessions, investments, cash, and properties owned by the individual or entity. Examples of assets include real estate, vehicles, bank accounts, stocks, bonds, jewelry, and more.

Total Liabilities: Liabilities encompass all debts, loans, and financial obligations that need to be repaid. This might include mortgages, car loans, credit card debts, personal loans, and any other outstanding payments.

Balance Sheet: A balance sheet is a financial statement that provides a snapshot of an individual's or organization's financial position at a specific point in time. It presents the assets, liabilities, and equity of the entity. A balance sheet follows the fundamental accounting equation:

ASSETS= LIABILITIES + EQUITY

Remember that a balance sheet should always balance, meaning that the total value of the assets should be equal to the combined value of the liabilities and equity. This ensures the accuracy of the financial information presented. Keep in mind that creating a complete and accurate balance sheet might involve more specific details and categories based on the individual's financial situation.

In the balance sheet:

The Assets section lists all the assets owned by the individual or entity, including cash, investments, properties, and more.

The Equity section represents the owner's equity or net worth, which is the difference between assets and liabilities.

NET WORTH STATEMENT

NAME		NET WORTH	-
DATE			

ASSETS (what you own)

CASH AND BANK ACCOUNTS — Amount

	Amount
Cash on hand	-
Cheque accounts	-
Savings accounts	-
Money market funds	-
Cash value of life insurance	-
Other (specify)	-
Other (specify)	-
Other (specify)	-
Other (specify)	-
TOTAL CASH AND BANK ACCOUNTS	**-**

INVESTMENTS (market value) — Amount

	Amount
Certificates of deposit	-
Stocks	-
Bonds	-
Mutual Funds	-
Annuities	-
IRAs	-
401(k), 403(b), 457 Plans	-
Pension Plan	-
Other (specify)	-
Other (specify)	-
Other (specify)	-
Other (specify)	-
TOTAL INVESTMENTS	**-**

PERSONAL PROPERTY (present value) — Amount

	Amount
Automobiles	-
Recreational Vehicle/Boat	-
Home Furnishings	-
Appliances and Furniture	-
Collections	-
Jewellery and Furs	-
Other (specify)	-
Other (specify)	
Other (specify)	-
Other (specify)	-
TOTAL PERSONAL PROPERTY	**-**
TOTAL ASSETS	**-**

19

OBTAINING A RESIDENTIAL

APPRAISAL FOR ESTATE

PLANNING

What is a residential appraisal?

A home appraisal is a third-party opinion of how much the home is worth based on the fair market value. During the appraisal process, a real estate appraiser will go to the home and take note of the home's condition, what repairs might be needed, and how it compares with other homes nearby that have recently sold. There are three approaches available to the appraiser in developing an opinion of value. First, there is the Cost Approach; this is determined by calculating the cost to construct the home. This approach is valid for a new construction or a home built in the last five years. The second approach is the Income Approach, which is determined by the calculated income the property produces, less expenses. The Last approach, and the one widely accepted by the Banks and for the purpose of establishing fair market value, is the Sales Comparison approach. In the Sales Comparison, the appraiser compares the subject home to recently sold homes to develop an opinion as to what the market is willing to pay for a similar home, having similar style, gross living area, features and amenities.

Here is a simple explanation of how it works:

Understand the Need for an Appraisal: The first step in the process is to recognize the need for an appraisal. Estate planning involves determining the value of your assets, such as real estate, personal property, investments, and more. This valuation is essential for various purposes, including tax planning, distributing assets, or setting up trusts.

Hire a Qualified Appraiser: To get an accurate appraisal, you'll need to hire a qualified appraiser. Look for individuals or firms with expertise in the specific type of assets you want to appraise. For instance, if you are dealing with real estate, you should hire a real estate appraiser. Ensure that the appraiser is certified and follows professional standards.

Gather information: Work closely with the appraiser to provide all necessary information about your home. This may include tax bills, financial records, receipts, photographs, and any relevant documentation. The more information you provide, the more accurate the appraisal will be.

Site Visits and Evaluation: The Appraiser will typically conduct site visits. For real estate, they will assess the property's condition, location, and market trends.

Market Research: Appraisers need to research the current market conditions and comparable sales to assess the fair market value of their assets. They use their expertise and industry knowledge to arrive at a well-informed valuation.

Report and Documentation: After completing the evaluation, the appraiser will provide you with a detailed report that includes their findings and the determined values of your assets. This report is a crucial document for your estate planning.

Use in Estate Planning: Once you have the appraisal report, you can use it for various estate planning purposes. This may involve determining how your assets will be distributed among your heirs, calculating potential estate taxes, or deciding whether you need to establish trusts to protect your wealth.

Consult with Legal and Financial Advisors: It's advisable to consult with legal and financial advisors as you incorporate the appraisal results into your estate planning strategy. They can help you make informed decisions and navigate any legal requirements or tax implications.

Update as Needed: Estate planning is an ongoing process. As your financial situation or asset portfolio changes, it's essential to periodically update your appraisals to ensure they remain accurate and relevant to your planning goals.

SUMMARY

In summary, getting an appraisal for estate planning involves hiring a qualified appraiser, assessing the value of your assets, and using that information to make informed decisions about the distribution of your wealth. Proper estate planning can help protect your assets, minimize taxes, and ensure your wishes are carried out effectively when you're no longer able to manage your estate yourself.

ESTATE PLANNING

Estate planning is making a plan for what happens to your things (property, money, and more after you pass away. It's like writing down instructions for who gets what and how they get it. This plan can help your family and loved ones know what to do when you're not around anymore, and it can also make sure that your wishes are followed.

Here are some of the key parts of estate planning.

Will: A will is a document where you say who gets your stuff when you die. You can also name someone to take care of your kids if they are still young.

Executor: This is the person you choose to make sure your wishes in your will are carried out. They handle things like paying your debts and distributing your assets.

Beneficiaries: These are the people who receive your assets. Like your money, life insurance payment, house, or other belongings, as per your instructions in your will or other documents.

Trust: You can create trusts to manage and distribute your assets in a specific way, like for education or taking care of a loved one with special needs.

Power of Attorney: You can choose someone to make decisions for you if you become unable to do so due to illness or injury.

Health Care Directive: This document lets you specify your medical wishes if you can't communicate them yourself. It helps your family make decisions about your healthcare.

Minimizing Taxes: Estate planning can also involve strategies to reduce the amount of taxes your heirs might have to pay on your assets

SUMMARY

Estate Planning isn't just for the wealthy; it is for anyone who wants to make things easier for their loved ones and ensure their wishes are respected. It's a way to provide peace of mind and protect your family's future. To get started, it's a good idea to consult with an attorney who specializes in estate planning to help you create a plan that suits your needs.

FICO SCORE

In today's modern financial landscape, credit scores play a pivotal role in shaping individuals' access to credit and financial opportunities. Among the various credit scoring models, the FICO score is widely recognized and utilized by lenders to assess an individual's creditworthiness. A FICO score reflects a person's credit history and serves as a numerical representation of their ability to manage credit responsibly. This essay delves into the concept of FICO scores, highlights their significance, and provides actionable strategies for improving them.

FICO score, developed by the Fair Isaac Corporation, is a credit scoring model that ranges from 300 to 850. It is calculated using several factors, each weighted differently.

PAYMENT HISTORY (35%)

This factor assesses an individual's track record of making payments on time. Delinquent payments, late payments, and accounts in collections can negatively impact this aspect of the score.

CREDIT UTILIZATION (30%)

This factor gauges the ratio of credit used to the total available credit limit. A lower credit utilization ratio is generally favorable, as it suggests responsible credit management.

LENGTH OF CREDIT IN USE (15%)

The length of time a person has held credit accounts influences their score. A longer credit history demonstrates stability and reliability.

TYPES OF CREDIT IN USE (10%)

A mix of credit accounts, such as credit cards, mortgages, and installment loans, can positively affect the score. It demonstrates the ability to manage different types of credit responsibly.

NEW CREDIT

Opening multiple new credit accounts within a short period can be perceived as risky behavior and may lower the score.

SIGNIFICANCE OF A FICO SCORES

FICO scores have far-reaching implications for individuals' financial lives.

LOAN APPROVAL

Lenders use FICO scores to evaluate loan applications. Higher scores increase the likelihood of loan approval and better interest rates, while lower scores can lead to rejection or higher borrowing costs.

INTEREST RATES

Individuals with higher FICO scores are offered lower interest rates, saving them substantial amounts over the life of a loan.

RENTAL APPLICATIONS

Landlords may check FICO scores during rental applications to assess potential tenants' financial reliability.

INSURANCE PREMIUMS

Some insurance companies consider FICO scores when determining premiums, as they view responsible financial behavior as indicative of responsible behavior in other areas of life.

STRATEGIES FOR IMPROVING FICO SCORES

Pay bills on time. Consistently paying bills by their due dates is the most effective way to enhance your payment history and boost your FICO score.

Reduce credit card balances. Lowering credit card balances relative to credit limits can significantly improve your credit utilization ratio.

Maintain a mix of credit types. Having a healthy mix of credit, such as credit cards and installment loans, showcases your ability to handle various financial obligations.

Keep old accounts open. The longer you establish your credit history, the better. Avoid closing old, well-managed accounts, as they contribute positively to your length of credit history.

Monitor your credit report. Regularly review your credit report for errors, fraudulent activities, or inaccuracies that might be negatively affecting your FICO score.

SUMMARY

FICO scores wield considerable influence over individuals' financial lives, impacting their access to credit, interest rates, and even opportunities such as renting an apartment or obtaining insurance. Understanding the factors that contribute to FICO scores and employing prudent financial practices can go a long way in improving them over time. By consistently making timely payments, managing credit responsibly, and adopting a proactive approach to credit management, individuals can enhance their FICO scores and unlock a wealth of financial opportunities.

HOMEOWNERS' INSURANCE

Homeowners Insurance plays a crucial role in safeguarding one's most valuable asset: their home. In the realm of homeowners insurance, there are three prominent policy types: Standard Fire, Named Peril, and All-Risk (also known as Open Peril) insurance policies. Each of these policies offers a distinct level of coverage and protection against various risks, and understanding their differences is essential for homeowners seeing to make informed decisions about their insurance needs.

STANDARD FIRE POLICY

The Standard Fire insurance policy is among the most basic and traditional types of homeowners insurance. It provides coverage against specific perils that are typically outlined in the policy, with the primary focus being on fire-related risks. This means that if a loss occurs due to a fire, the homeowner is entitled to compensation for damages up to the policy's limits. However, this coverage is often limited to fire-related damages and may not extend to other perils, such as theft, vandalism, or natural disasters. Standard Fire insurance is a budget-friendly option for those seeking to cover their home against a limited number of risks.

NAMED PERIL POLICY

A NAMED Peril insurance policy takes coverage a step further by providing protection against a predetermined list of perils explicitly mentioned in the policy. These perils might include events like lightning, hail, windstorms, theft, vandalism, and other specific risks. If a loss occurs due to one of the named perils, the homeowner is eligible for compensation. However, if a loss arises from a peril not listed in the policy, the homeowner would not be covered. Named Peril insurance offers more comprehensive coverage than Standard Fire insurance policy but still has limitations based on specific risks.

ALL-RISK POLICY

The all-Risk Insurance policy is often considered the most comprehensive and inclusive type of homeowners insurance. Unlike Standard Fire and Named Peril policies, an All-Risk policy covers a wide range of perils by default, unless a specific peril is explicitly excluded. This "all-risk" approach means that the burden of proof lies with the insurer to demonstrate that a particular event is not covered, rather than with the homeowner to prove that it is. While certain high-risk perils, like earthquakes and floods, might still require separate endorsements, an All-Risk policy provides a significantly broader scope of protection, making it the preferred choice for many homeowners who want extensive coverage.

SUMMARY

In conclusion, the distinctions between Standard Fire, Named Peril, and All-Risk homeowner's insurance policies lie in the level of coverage they offer and the range of perils they protect against. Standard Fire insurance provides basic protection against fire-related damages, Named Peril insurance extends coverage to a specified list of risks, and All-Risk insurance offers the most comprehensive protection by default, excluding only explicitly excluded perils. Homeowners should carefully assess their needs, budget, and risk profile to determine which type of policy aligns best with their circumstances. Making an informed decision can ensure that homeowners have the peace of mind they deserve, knowing their most valuable asset is adequately protected against potential loss.

Filing a peril loss on a homeowners' insurance policy involves the following steps:

ASSESS THE DAMAGE: Determine the extent of the damage or loss to your property caused by a covered peril. Covered perils typically include events like fires, storms, theft, and vandalism.

REVIEW YOUR POLICY: Carefully read your homeowners' insurance policy to understand what perils are covered and what the terms and conditions are for filing a claim. This will help you know whether the damage is eligible for coverage.

CONTACT YOUR INSURANCE COMPANY: Notify your insurance company about the damage as soon as possible. Most insurers have a specific claims hotline or online portal for this purpose. Be ready to provide details about the damage, including the date and cause of the loss.

DOCUMENT THE DAMAGE; Take clear photographs or videos of the damage to provide visual evidence of the loss. This documentation can be crucial when assessing the claim.

PREVENT FURTHER DAMAGE: If possible, take reasonable steps to prevent further damage. This might include things like placing a tarp on a leaking roof or boarding up broken windows. Document these temporary repairs as well, as they might be reimbursable.

FILE A CLAIM FORM: Your insurance company will guide you through the claims process, which often involves filling out a claims form. Provide accurate and complete information to facilitate the process.

PROVIDE DOCUMENTATION: Along with the claim form, you may need to submit evidence of ownership (receipts, photos), estimates for repairs or replacements, and any other relevant information as requested by your insurer.

ADJUSTER'S VISIT: In some cases, an insurance adjuster will visit your property to assess the damage in person. They will determine the extent of the loss and its coverage under your policy.

RECEIVE CLAIM DECISION: After reviewing the information and assessing the damage, your insurance company will provide you with a claim decision. This could involve approving the claim partially or in full, or in some cases, denying the claim.

REPAIR OR REPLACE: If your claim is approved, work with the insurance company to determine the next steps for repairing or replacing the damaged property. They might issue a check for the estimated cost of repairs, or they might work directly with contractors for repairs.

DEDUCTIBLE AND PAYMENT: Keep in mind that you will likely have to pay a deductible before the insurance coverage kicks in. The insurance company will provide you with the appropriate payment based on the terms of your policy.

CLAIM CLOSURE: Once repairs or replacements are completed, your claim will be closed. Ensure that you're satisfied with the work done before signing off on the claim closure.

Remember to keep all communication and documentation related to your claim in case you need them in the future. It's also a good idea to maintain a good working relationship with your insurance company throughout the process to ensure a smooth claims experience.

LIFE INSURANCE

Life Insurance plays a crucial role in managing financial risks and providing security to individuals and their families. Among the various types of life insurance, three prominent options are whole life insurance, universal life insurance, and term insurance.

Each of these insurance types serves distinct purposes, offers unique benefits, and caters to different financial needs. This essay aims to provide a comprehensive comparison of whole life insurance, universal life insurance, and term insurance, highlighting their key differences.

WHOLE LIFE INSURANCE

Whole life insurance is a permanent life insurance policy that provides coverage for the entire lifetime of the insured individual. It combines a death benefit with a savings or investment component, known as cash value.

Premiums for whole life insurance are generally higher than those for term insurance due to the lifelong coverage and the cash value accumulation. The cash value grows over time at a predetermined rate and can be borrowed against or withdrawn for various purposes. Whole life insurance offers a guaranteed death benefit and predictable premium payments, making it a stable option for individuals seeking lifelong protection and a savings element.

UNIVERSAL LIFE INSURANCE

Universal life insurance is another form of permanent life insurance that offers greater flexibility compared to whole life insurance. It provides a death benefit along with a cash value component, similar to whole life insurance. However, the distinguishing feature of universal life insurance is the ability to adjust the premium payments and death benefits, within certain limits, based on changes in the policyholder's financial situation and needs.

The policyholder can also invest the cash value in a variety of investment options, potentially leading to higher returns. Universal life insurance allows policyholders to increase or decrease their coverage, change premium payment schedules, and even skip payments, making it a versatile choice for those seeking adaptable life insurance coverage.

TERM INSURANCE

Term insurance is a type of life insurance that provides coverage for a specific period, or term, which can range from 5 to 30 years or more. Unlike permanent insurance, term insurance does not accumulate cash value and only offers a death benefit.

Premiums for term insurance are generally lower than those for permanent insurance, making it an affordable option for individuals who want coverage for a defined period, such as when their dependents are young or during mortgage-paying years. Term insurance is suitable for those seeking temporary financial protection and not necessarily an investment component.

ANALYSIS

COVERAGE PERIOD: Whole life and universal life insurance provide lifelong coverage, while term insurance covers a specific period.

PREMIUMS: Whole life insurance has higher premiums due to its permanent coverage and cash value component. Universal life insurance offers more flexibility in premium payments, and term insurance is low.

CASH VALUE: Both whole life and universal life insurance build cash value over time, whereas term insurance does not accumulate cash

INVESTMENT COMPONENT: Universal life insurance offers investment options for policyholders, unlike whole life and term.

FLEXIBILITY: Universal life insurance is the most flexible, allowing policyholders to adjust premiums and death benefits. Term insurance is fixed for the term, while whole life insurance has less flexibility than universal life.

DEATH BENEFITS: All three types offer a death benefit, with whole life and universal life insurance having guaranteed death benefits, while term insurance provides a death benefit only during the term.

CONCLUSION

Choosing the right life insurance depends on individual financial goals and circumstances. Whole life insurance offers lifelong protection and a cash value component. Universal life insurance provides flexibility in premiums and coverage adjustments, along with investment options. Term insurance is suitable for temporary coverage needs with lower premiums. By understanding the differences between whole life, universal life, and term insurance, individuals can make informed decisions that align with their financial objectives and security requirements,

Filing for a death benefits under your life insurance policy, follow these steps:

NOTIFY THE INSURANCE COMPANY: When the policyholder (the person whose life was insured) passes away, the beneficiary or their representative needs to contact the insurance company as soon as possible. This can usually be done through a phone call to the insurance company's customer service department. The insurer will guide through the rest of the steps.

GATHER THE REQUIRED DOCUMENTATION: The insurance company will provide you with a list of documents that you need to submit to initiate the death benefit claim. These documents usually include the policyholder's death certificate, a claim form provided by the insurer, and any other relevant paperwork that the company requires.

COMPLETE THE CLAIM FORM: You will need to fill out a claim form provided by the insurance company. This form gathers important information about the policyholder, the beneficiary, and the circumstances surrounding the death.

SUBMIT THE DOCUMENTATION: Compile all the necessary documents, including the completed claim form and a copy of the policyholder's death certificate. Make sure all the information is accurate and complete. You can send these documents to the insurance company either electronically or through the mail, as per their instructions.

REVIEW AND VERIFICATION: The insurance company will review the submitted documents to ensure that everything is in order. They might also conduct a thorough review of the policy to confirm its validity and the terms of coverage.

PROCESSING: Once the documents are verified and approved, the insurance company will begin processing the death benefit claim. This process involves calculating the amount of the benefit based on the terms of the policy.

DISBURSEMENT: After processing is complete, the insurance company will issue the death benefit payout to the designated beneficiary or beneficiaries. This payout can take various forms, such as a lump sum payment, annuity, or other agreed-upon arrangements.

TAX CONSIDERATIONS: It's important to note that while life insurance death benefits are typically not subject to income tax, they might be subject to estate tax in some cases. Consult with a tax professional to understand the implications for your specific situation.

Keep in mind, the exact process and requirements might vary depending on the insurance company and the specific policy. It's recommended to communicate directly with your insurance provider to understand their procedures for filing a death benefit claim.

AUTOMOBILE INSURANCE

An auto insurance policy is a contract between an individual and an insurance company that provides financial protection in case of accidents or damage to a vehicle. Understanding the components of an auto policy is crucial for making informed decisions and ensuring proper coverage. This summary outlines the key elements of an auto policy breakdown.

Liability Coverage: Liability coverage is mandated in most states and covers the policyholder's legal responsibility for bodily injury and property damage to others in an accident. It is divided into two parts:

Bodily Injury Liability: Liability coverage is mandated in most states and covers the policyholder's legal responsibility for bodily injury and property damage to others in an accident.

Property Damage Liability: Covers the cost of repairing or replacing another person's property (e.g., vehicles, buildings) damaged in an accident.

Collision Coverage: Collision coverage pays for the repair or replacement of the policyholder's vehicle in case of a collision, regardless of who is at fault. Deductibles apply, and coverage limits depend on the vehicle's current value.

Comprehensive Coverage: Comprehensive coverage protects against non-collision events such as theft, vandalism, natural disasters, and animal collisions. Like collision coverage, comprehensive coverage also comes with deductibles and coverage limits based on the vehicle's value.

Personal Injury Protection (PIP) or Medical Payments: These coverages provide medical expenses for the policyholder and passengers in their vehicle, regardless of fault. PIP may also cover additional costs like lost wages and funeral expenses. Coverage varies by state.

Uninsured/Underinsured Motorist Coverage: This coverage safeguards the policyholder if they're in an accident with a driver who has insufficient or no insurance. It covers medical expenses and, in some cases, property damage.

Deductibles: Deductibles are the amount the policyholder agrees to pay out of pocket before the insurance coverage kicks in. Higher deductibles often lead to lower premium costs but require more payment upfront in case of a claim.

Premiums: Premiums are the regular payments made by the policyholder to maintain insurance coverage. They're determined by factors such as the driver's age, driving record, city or state, type of coverage, and the vehicle's make and model.

Policy Limits: Policy limits refer to the maximum amount the insurance company will pay for a claim. It's important to select adequate coverage limits to ensure sufficient financial protection in case of a major accident.

Additional Coverage: Policyholders can often add extras like rental car coverage, roadside assistance, and gap insurance (covers the difference between the car's value and the amount owed on a loan or lease.

SUMMARY

In conclusion, an auto policy is a multi-faceted contract designed to provide financial security in various scenarios. By understanding the breakdown of an auto policy, individuals can make informed decisions when choosing coverage options and tailoring their policies to meet their specific needs. Regularly reviewing and updating the policy is essential to ensure continued protection and peace of mind on the road.

Here's a simple step-by-step guide on how to file an automobile claim:

SAFETY FIRST: Ensure everyone involved in the accident is safe. If there are injuries, call for medical assistance immediately. If the vehicles are obstructing traffic, consider moving them to a safer location if possible.

CONTACT AUTHORITIES: Depending on the severity of the accident, you might need to call the police to the scene. They will create an official report which can be useful when filing your claim.

GATHER INFORMATION: Exchange contact, insurance, and driver's license details with the other parties involved in the accident. Also, note down the license plate numbers, makes, models, and colors of all vehicles involved.

DOCUMENT THE SCENE: If it's safe, take pictures of the accident scene, including vehicle damage, license plates, the positions of vehicles, and any relevant road signs or signals. This visual evidence can be helpful when making your claim.

NOTIFY YOUR INSURANCE COMPANY: When talking to your insurance company, be honest and accurate in your description of the accident. Avoid speculating or admitting fault, as the claims process will involve an investigation.

FILE A CLAIM FORM: The insurance company might assign an adjuster to investigate the claim. Cooperate fully by providing any requested documents, statements, or evidence related to the accident.

COOPERATE WITH THE INVESTIGATION: Your insurance company might assign an adjuster to investigate the claim. Cooperate fully by providing any requested documents, statements, or evidence related to the accident. If you are the adverse party you may want to consult the advice of an attorney before speaking with the other insurance company or representative.

GET REPAIR ESTIMATES: If your vehicle is damaged, the insurance company might require you to get repair estimates. This helps them determine the cost of repairs or whether the vehicle is a total loss.

MEDICAL CLAIMS: If you or any passengers were injured, you'll need to file a medical claim as well. Provide the insurance company with medical records, bills, and any other relevant information.

KEEP RECORDS: Throughout the claims process, keep copies of all communication with your insurance company, including emails, letters, and claim numbers. If you were injured in the accident keep a journal of the extent and treatment.

SETTLEMENT: Depending on the investigation's findings and the terms of your policy, the insurance company will offer a settlement. If you agree with the settlement, they will proceed with the payment process. If, you feel that the settlement offer is inadequate you may want to seek the advice of an attorney.

Keep in mind, the process can vary depending on your insurance policy, location, and the specifics of the accident. It's always a good idea to review your insurance policy and familiarize yourself with the claims process beforehand, so you know what to expect.

SECURING A HOME LOAN OR MORTGAGE

Securing a home loan or mortgage is a significant financial decision, and lenders have certain requirements to ensure that borrowers are qualified and capable of repaying the loan. Here's what. a person typically needs to secure a home loan or mortgage.

GOOD CREDIT SCORE

A strong credit score is crucial. It indicates your creditworthiness and history of managing credit. Lenders use this score to assess the risk of lending to you. Generally, a higher credit score improves your chances of getting approved for a mortgage and can also lead to better-to-better interest rates.

STABLE INCOME

Lenders want to see that you have a reliable source of income to make regular mortgage payments. Typically, you'll need to provide proof of employment, income statements (such as pay stubs or tax returns), and possibly verification of other sources of income.

DOWN PAYMENT

You'll need to put down a certain percentage of the home's purchase price as a down payment. The exact percentage varies, but it's usually around 20%. A larger down payment can often lead to more favorable loan terms.

DEBT-TO-INCOME (DTI)

Lenders assess your debt-to-income ratio, which compares your monthly debt payments (including the prospective mortgage payment) to your gross monthly income. A lower DTI ratio is generally preferred, as it indicates you have enough income to cover your debts.

PROOF OF ASSETS

Lenders may require you to provide documentation of your assets, such as bank statements, investment accounts, and retirement accounts. This shows that you have the financial resources to cover the down payment, closing costs, and other expenses.

EMPLOYMENT HISTORY

A stable employment history demonstrates your ability to maintain a consistent income. Lenders often look for a history of steady employment over the past two years.

DOCUMENTATION

You will need to provide various documents, such as your identification (passport, driver's license, etc.), Social Security number, proof of residency, and any legal documents related to your financial situation.

PROPERTY INFORMATION

If you've already chosen a property, the lender will need details about it, including the address, purchase price, and property type. The lender might also require an appraisal to assess the property's value.

LOAN APPLICATION

You'll need to fill out a mortgage application, providing details about your finances, employment, and the property you intend to purchase.

MORTGAGE PRE-APPROVAL

Before you start house hunting, getting pre-approved for a mortgage is beneficial. Pre-approval gives you an estimate of how much you can afford, making your search more focused and showing sellers that you're a serious buyer.

CREDIT HISTORY REPORT

Lenders will review your credit history and obtain a credit report to assess your creditworthiness. Make sure your credit report is accurate, and dispute any errors if necessary.

INSURANCE

Lenders typically require homeowners' insurance to protect their investment in case of damage or loss to the property.

STOCKS

What is a stock? A stock represents a tiny piece of ownership in a company. Imagine a pizza; a stock is like one slice of that of that pizza.

Why do companies offer stocks? Companies sell stocks to raise money. This money helps them grow their business, build new products, or expand.

Buying stocks: When you buy a stock, you're essentially buying a share of that company. You hope that the company will do well, and the value of your stock will increase.

Selling stocks: You can sell your stocks whenever you want, ideally when their value has gone up. This is how you make a profit.

Stock prices: Stock prices go up and down. They're influenced by how well the company is doing, the economy, and other factors. Think of it like a see-saw; it can tilt one way or the other.

Stock Market: The stock market is like a giant auction house where people buy and sell stocks. The most famous stock market is the New York Stock Exchange. (NYSE) and (Nasdaq), National Association of Securities Dealers Automated Quotations.

Investing vs. Trading: Many investor's strategy is to buy stocks and hold them for a long time, hoping they'll become more valuable over the years (that's investing). Others buy and sell stocks quickly to try and make quick profits (that's trading).

Risks: Investing in stocks carries risks. If the company doesn't do well, the value of your stock can go down, and you might lose all of your initial investment.

Diversification: To reduce risk, many people spread their money across different stocks and even other investments like bonds or real estate. This is called diversification. Mutual Funds are a great way to diversify our stock portfolio.

MUTUAL FUNDS AND ETF'S

Mutual Funds: What are they? Mutual funds are like big baskets of investments. They pool money from many investors to buy a diverse mix of stocks, bonds, and other assets. Mutual funds allow you to invest in specific segments of the market, such as energy, health care or technology.

How they work: When you invest in a mutual fund, you buy shares of the fund itself, not the individual assets inside it. Your money is managed by professional fund managers who make investments on behalf of the fund.

Pros: Diversification (spreading risk, professional management, easy for beginners.

Cons: Often have higher fees (expense ratios), typically trade once a day after the markets have closed.

Exchange-Traded Funds (ETFs): What are they? ETFs are similar to mutual funds but are traded on the stock exchange, just like individual stocks.

How they work: When you buy an ETF, you're purchasing shares of a fund that holds a variety of assets (like stocks, bonds, or commodities). ETF prices change throughout the trading day as they are bought and sold.

Pros: Diversification, often lower fees than mutual funds, can be bought and sold throughout the day like stocks.

Cons: Cost of buying and selling shares.

SUMMARY

To sum it up, both Mutual funds and ETFs allow you to invest in a diversified portfolio without having to select individual investments yourself. Mutual funds are usually bought and sold through the fund company at the day's closing price, while ETFs are traded on stock exchanges like individual stocks throughout the trading day. Your choice between them often depends on your investment style, goals, preferences and risk tolerance.

BONDS

Think of a bond as a special type of loan. Imagine you have some money, and a company or the government needs to borrow money. They issue bonds as a way to borrow from people like you. When you buy a bond, you're actually lending your money to the company or government.

HOW BONDS WORK

Issuing Bonds: Let's say a company needs $1,000. Instead of borrowing from a bank, they decide to borrow from individuals like you. They create bonds, each worth $100. So, they issue 10 bonds in total.

Buying Bonds: You decide to buy one of those $100 bonds. You're essentially giving the company $100.

Interest: In return for lending your money, the company promises to pay you interest regularly. This is like a thank-you for letting them use your money. For instance, they might promise to pay you 5% interest every year.

Bond life: Bonds have an expiration date, just like food has an expiration date. When the bond "matures," it means the time is up.

So, if the company sets the maturity period at 5 years, after 5 years, they will give you back your initial $100.

Getting paid back: In addition, to the initial invested amount, you also receive back the interest they promised. In this case, 5% interest on $100 is $5 per year. So, over 5 years, you'd receive $25 in interest payments.

SUMMARY

To sum it up, a bond is like lending money to a company or government. You get your money back when the bond matures, along with some extra money as interest for letting them borrow from you.

People like bonds because they are usually safer investments compared to stocks. However, there's still some risk involved, especially if the company or government faces financial trouble. Always remember that investing involves risks, and it's important to do your research or consult a financial advisor before making any decisions.

ANNUITIES

An annuity is a financial product that involves a series of regular payments or receipts made at consistent intervals over a specified period of time. It's like a regular income stream that can be used for retirement planning, savings, or investments. Annuities can be thought of as the opposite of a loan, where instead of borrowing money and paying it back over time, you invest money and receive periodic payments in return.

There are two main types of annuities.

FIXED ANNUITIES

In a fixed annuity, you invest a lump sum with an insurance company or financial institution. They promise to pay you a fixed amount of money at regular intervals, typically monthly, quarterly, or annually. The payments remain the same throughout the agreed-upon period, providing you with a predictable income source.

VARIABLE ANNUITIES

With a variable annuity, your investment is typically placed in a variety of investment options, such as stocks, bonds, or mutual funds. The payments you receive can vary based on the performance of these underlying investments. This type of annuity carries more risk compared to a fixed annuity, but it also offers the potential for higher returns.

Annuities can be used for retirement planning, as they can provide a steady income during your retirement years. They're also often used for long-term savings goals or for creating a guaranteed income stream for a specific period.

Remember that annuities can have various terms, fees, and features, so it's important to carefully read the contract and understand the terms before committing to one. It's also recommended to consult with a financial advisor to determine if an annuity is a suitable option for your financial goals.

CREDIT UNION

AN ALTERNATIVE TO BANKS

Ownership and Membership: Credit unions are member-owned. This means the people who use the credit union's services are also the owners.

To be a member, you typically need to meet certain eligibility criteria, such as living in a specific geographic area or working for a particular employer. These criteria vary from one credit union to another.

Not-for-profit Structure: Credit unions are not-for-profit organizations. This means they don't aim to make a profit for shareholders but instead focus on providing financial services to their members at their best possible terms.

Any profits earned are usually reinvested into the credit union or returned to members in the form of better interest rates and lower fees.

Services offered: Credit unions offer a wide range of services similar to banks. These services typically include saving accounts, checking accounts, personal loans, mortgages and more.

Credit unions often emphasize personal service and a sense of community, as they are owned and operated by members who share common interests.

Governance: Credit unions are democratically run. Members elect a board of directors from among the members to oversee the credit union's operations and make important decisions.

This democratic structure ensures that the credit union's policies and practices align with the needs and preferences of its members.

Competitive Rates: Credit unions often offer competitive interest rates on savings accounts and lower interest on personal loans and credit cards compared to traditional banks.

This can result in cost savings for the members when borrowing money or earning interest on their savings.

Federally Insured: Like banks, which are regulated and insured, credit unions are regulated and insured as well. Many of the credit unions are incurred by the National Credit Union Administration (NCUA), which provides a level of security for their member's deposits.

SUMMARY

Credit unions offer another alternative to traditional banks. Many employers have employee-run credit unions available to their employees as a way to offer them financial services and competitive interest rates. If you have access to become a member of a credit union, it is a prudent plan to become a member.

CRYPTOCURRENCY

Cryptocurrency is a type of digital or virtual currency that uses cryptography for security. Here's a simple explanation:

Digital Money: Think of cryptocurrency as money, just like the dollars or euros in your wallet, but it only exists in digital form. There are no physical coins or bills.

Decentralized: Unlike traditional currencies that are controlled by governments and banks, cryptocurrencies operate on a technology called blockchain. This is like a public ledger that records all transactions, and it's not owned or controlled by any single entity. Instead, it's maintained by a network of computers (nodes).

Cryptography: Cryptocurrencies use advanced math and computer science techniques to secure transactions and control the creation of new units. This makes it very difficult for anyone to cheat or counterfeit.

Ownership: When you own cryptocurrency, you have a digital wallet that contains your coins. This wallet is secured with a private key, which is like a super-secret password. Only the person with the private key can access and use the cryptocurrency.

Transactions: When you want to send cryptocurrency to someone, you create a digital transaction. This transaction is added to the blockchain and verified by the network of computers. Once verified, the recipient gets the cryptocurrency, and it's recorded on the blockchain.

Volatility: Cryptocurrency prices can be highly volatile. This means their value can go up and down dramatically in a short period. It's a bit like the stock market but operates 24/7.

Application: People use cryptocurrencies for various purposes, including as a digital investment (like buying stocks), for online purchases, and even for transferring money internationally quickly and with potentially lower fees than traditional banks.

SUMMARY

To sum it up, cryptocurrencies are digital, decentralized, and secure forms of money that rely on cryptography and a public ledger (blockchain) to function. They offer new ways of handling financial transactions and investments in the digital age.

401(K)

RETIREMENT SAVINGS

ACCOUNT:

ENROLLMENT: When you start a job with a company that offers a 401(k) plan, you have the option to enroll in the plan. You'll need to complete some paperwork to set up your account.

CONTRIBUTIONS: Once enrolled, you can decide how much money you want to contribute from your paycheck to your 401(k) account. This contribution is deducted from your pre-tax income, meaning the money is taken out before taxes are calculated. This reduces your taxable income for the year, potentially lowering your tax bill.

EMPLOYER MATCH: Some employers offer a matching contribution, where they'll contribute a certain percentage of your salary to your 401(k) account as well. For example, if your employer offers a 50% match and you contribute $100, they'll add $50 to your account. This is essentially free money for your retirement savings.

INVESTMENT OPTIONS: Inside your 401(k) account, you'll have a range of investment options to choose from. These could include stocks, bonds, mutual funds, and more. Your contributions are invested based on your choices, with the goal of growing your savings over time.

TAX ADVANTAGES: One of the main benefits of a 401(k) is its tax advantages. Not only are your contributions made with pre-tax income, but any investment gains within the account are also tax-deferred. This means you won't pay taxes on the growth until you withdraw the money in retirement.

VESTING: Your contributions are always 100% yours. However, employer contributions might be subject to a vesting schedule. Vesting determines how much of the employer-contributed funds you actually own if you leave the company before a certain period. Over time, you'll become fully vested, and all the employer-contributed money will be yours.

WITHDRAWALS: The purpose of a 401(k) is to save for retirement, so there are rules about when you can withdraw the money without penalties. Generally, you can start taking penalty-free withdrawals at age 59½. If you withdraw before this age, you might incur taxes and an additional early withdrawal penalty.

REQUIRED MINIMUM DISTRIBUTION: Once you reach age 72 (formerly 70½), the government requires you to start taking minimum distributions from your 401(k) to ensure that you don't defer taxes indefinitely.

PORTABILITY: If you change jobs, you won't lose your 401(k) savings. You can roll over your existing 401(k) balance into a new employer's plan or an Individual Retirement Account (IRA).

Keep in mind, that a 401(k) plan is a valuable tool for building a secure retirement. It allows you to save money from your paycheck before taxes, benefit from potential employer contributions, invest for growth, and take advantage of tax benefits while following certain rules to ensure your savings are used for retirement.

INDIVIDUAL RETIREMENT ACCOUNT(S)

TRADITIONAL INDIVIDUAL RETIREMENT ACCOUNT: A traditional IRA is a type of retirement savings account that provides individuals with a tax-advantaged way to save for their retirement. Here's how it works:

CONTRIBUTIONS: You can contribute a certain amount of your earnings each year to your Traditional IRA, up to a maximum limit set by the IRS. These contributions are typically tax-deductible, meaning they can reduce your taxable income for the year in which you make the contribution. This can provide you with an immediate tax benefit.

INVESTEMENTS: Once the money is in your Traditional IRA, you can invest it in various financial instruments like stocks, bonds, mutual funds, and more. The investments have the potential to grow over time, allowing your retirement savings to increase potentially.

TAXATION: The contributions and any investment earnings in a Traditional IRA grow tax-deferred. This means you don't pay taxes on the gains or interest until you start withdrawing the money.

WITHDRAWALS: When you retire and start withdrawing money from your Traditional IRA, the withdrawals are treated as ordinary income and are subject to income tax at your current tax rate. This tax treatment assumes you're withdrawing the money after reaching the age of 59½. If you withdraw money before this age, you might be subject to early withdrawal penalties and taxes.

ROTH INDIVIDUAL RETIREMENT ACCOUNT: A Roth IRA is another type of retirement savings account, but with a different tax structure. Here's how it works:

CONTRIBUTIONS: Similar to a Traditional IRA, you can contribute a certain amount of your earnings each year to your Roth IRA, up to the IRS-set limit. However, the contributions you make to a Roth IRA are not tax-deductible, so they won't lower your current taxable income.

INVESTEMENTS: Just like a Traditional IRA, you can invest the money within your Roth IRA in various financial assets to potentially grow your savings over time.

TAXATION: The key difference with a Roth IRA is that contributions are made with after-tax money, which means you've already paid taxes on the income you contribute. The big advantage here is that qualified withdrawals, including both contributions and earnings, are tax-free. This means that when you retire and start withdrawing money, you won't owe any additional income tax,

WITHDRAWALS: Another advantage of a Roth IRA is flexibility. You can generally withdraw your contributions (not the earnings) at any time without penalties or taxes. However, to take advantage of the tax-free treatment of earnings, you usually need to be at least 59½ and have held the Roth IRA for at least five years.

Keep in mind, that both Traditional and Roth IRAs offer tax advantages for retirement savings, but they differ in terms of when you get the tax benefits (Traditional IRA gives you immediate tax deductions, Roth IRA gives you tax-free withdrawals in retirement) and how withdrawals are taxed. The

choice between the two often depends on your current financial situation, expected future tax rates, and individual retirement goals. It's a good idea to consult with a financial advisor to determine which type of IRA suits your needs best.

REAL ESTATE

Real Estate ownership has long been considered one of the most reliable and lucrative investments available. The allure of owning property extends beyond the immediate benefits of shelter; it encompasses a wide range of advantages that contribute to personal financial growth and security. This essay explores the multifaceted advantages of owning real estate, ranging from potential capital appreciation and passive income to tax benefits and portfolio diversification.

Capital Appreciation: One of the primary advantages of owning real estate is the potential for capital appreciation. Over time, well-located properties tend to increase in value due to factors such as population growth, urbanization, and economic development. While real estate markets can experience fluctuations, historical trends suggest a general upward trajectory. Property owners who hold onto their investments for an extended period can benefit from substantial gains when they decide to sell.

Passive Income: Real estate ownership provides the opportunity for generating passive income through rental properties. Owning rental properties allows investors to earn a consistent stream of income from monthly rent payments. This income can help cover mortgage payments, and property maintenance costs, and potentially provide a surplus that contributes to the owner's overall financial stability. Rental income can serve as an alternative source of income, offering a degree of financial security even during economic downturns.

Tax Benefits: Real estate ownership offers several tax advantages that can significantly impact an individual's financial situation. Mortgage interest payments and property taxes are often deductible from taxable income. Additionally, in many jurisdictions, rental property owners can deduct expenses related to property management, maintenance, and repairs. Depreciation of the property's value over time can also provide tax benefits, effectively reducing the amount of taxable rental income.

Portfolio Diversification: Real estate allows individuals to diversify their investment portfolios beyond traditional assets like stocks and bonds. Real estate often demonstrates a lower correlation with the performance of these traditional assets, which means that when the value of stocks and bonds declines, the value of real estate may remain relatively stable or even appreciated. This diversification can provide a degree of protection against market volatility and reduce overall investment risk.

Hedge Against Inflation: Real estate ownership can act as a hedge against inflation. As the cost-of-living increases over time, the value of real estate tends to rise as well. This means that rental income and the value of the property itself can increase in response to inflation, helping property owners maintain their purchasing power and financial well-being.

SUMMARY

Owning Real estate offers a plethora of advantages that extend far beyond the basic need for shelter. From potential capital appreciation and the generation of passive income to tax benefits and portfolio diversification, real estate ownership has the power to significantly impact an individual's financial standing. While, like any investment, it comes with its own set of risks and considerations, the benefits it provides have established it as a cornerstone of wealth-building and financial security for generations.

INVESTING IN GOLD AND SILVER

Investing in gold and silver can be a valuable addition to your investment strategy for several reasons:

Diversification: Gold and silver are considered "safe-haven" assets because they tend to retain their value or even appreciate during times of economic uncertainty or market volatility. By adding these precious metals to your portfolio, you can diversify your investments and reduce overall risk.

Hedge Against Inflation: Gold and silver historically have acted as a hedge against inflation. When the purchasing power of fiat currencies decreases due to rising inflation, the value of precious metals often increases. Holding gold and silver can help protect your wealth from the erosive effects of inflation.

Store of Value: Gold and silver have been used as a store of value for thousands of years. Unlike paper currency, which can lose value over time, these metals have maintained their worth. They are tangible assets that can be held physically, which can provide a sense of security in uncertain times.

Portfolio Stability: Gold and silver tend to have a low or negative correlation with other asset classes, such as stocks and bonds. This means that when other investments are performing poorly, the value of gold and silver may rise, helping to stabilize your portfolio's overall returns.

Long-Term Wealth Preservation: Historically, gold and silver have maintained their value over the long term. While they may experience short-term fluctuations, their overall trend has been one of appreciation, making them attractive for investors looking to preserve wealth for future generations.

Liquidity: Precious metals are highly liquid assets. You can easily buy and sell them through various channels, such as bullion dealers, jewelry stores, or online platforms. This liquidity ensures that you can access your investment when needed.

Tangible Asset: Unlike many financial assets that exist only in digital or paper form, gold and silver are physical assets that you can hold in your hand. This tangibility can provide a sense of security, as you have a physical representation of your investment.

SUMMARY

It is important to note that while gold and silver can be valuable additions to your portfolio, they also come with risks and considerations. Prices can be volatile, and they don't generate income like stocks or bonds. Additionally, storage and security can be a concern, especially for larger quantities. As with any investment, it's crucial to do your research, assess your financial goals, and consider your risk tolerance before deciding to invest in gold and silver. It's also advisable to consult with a financial advisor for personalized guidance on incorporating precious metals into your investment strategy.

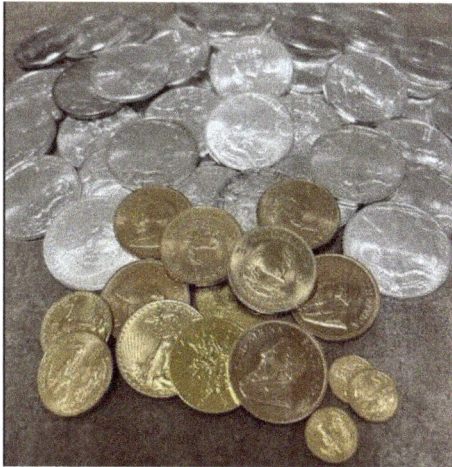

THE POWER OF GOAL SETTING

Goal setting is a fundamental process that allows individuals to define their aspirations, create a roadmap for success, and, ultimately, transform their dreams into reality. Whether it's in the realm of personal development, career advancement, or any other aspect of life, setting goals provides direction, motivation, and a sense of purpose.

The Importance of Setting Goals:

Clarity and Focus: Goals provide us with a clear target to aim for. They help us identify what we want to achieve and, in turn, allow us to concentrate our efforts and resources on what truly matters. Without goals, we may drift aimlessly, lacking direction and purpose.

Motivation: Setting goals gives us something to strive for, igniting our motivation and driving us to take action. When we have a compelling reason to work towards an objective, we are more likely to stay committed, even when faced with obstacles or setbacks.

Time Management: Goal setting forces us to prioritize tasks and allocate our time and resources efficiently. It helps us identify which activities are essential and which are distractions, leading to improved time management skills.

Overcoming Procrastination: Goals create a sense of urgency, encouraging us to take action today rather than putting things off till later. When we have a specific deadline or target in mind, we are less likely to procrastinate.

Measure of Success: Goals act as benchmarks for success. They enable us to measure our progress and determine whether we are on track to achieve our desired outcomes. This sense of accomplishment can boost our self-esteem and confidence.

Be smart when setting goals; follow these guidelines:

Specific: Goals should be clearly defined and specific. Vague objectives are difficult to pursue because they lack clarity.

Measurable: Goals should include specific criteria that allow you to measure your progress and determine if you have achieved them.

Relevant: Goals should be relevant to your overall objectives and aligned with your values and priorities.

Achievable: Goals should be realistic and attainable, given our current resources and capabilities.

SUMMARY

In conclusion, goal setting is a powerful tool that empowers individuals to shape their future and achieve their dreams. It provides clarity, motivation, and a roadmap to success. Whether pursuing short-term or long-term goals, following these guidelines can help you reach your goals.

CLOSING PROMOTION

In closing, I want to express my sincere gratitude for joining me on this journey through "Taking the First Step to Financial Security: A Primer on Financial Literacy." I hope that the knowledge and insights you've gained from this book have empowered you to take control of your financial future.

As we conclude this chapter, I'm excited to announce my next book, "Taking the Next Step to Walking towards Wealth." In this upcoming exploration, we will delve deeper into the fascinating world of financial strategies, including exotic stock options, call-and-put options, and other innovative techniques that can accelerate your path to wealth.

The journey doesn't end here; it's only just begun. With the right tools and knowledge, you can transform your financial dreams into reality. So, keep your eyes peeled for *"Taking the Next Step to Walking towards Wealth,"* and let's continue this exciting journey together toward financial prosperity.

Thank you for your support and dedication to your financial well-being. Remember, the journey to wealth is a marathon, not a sprint, and you've already taken that crucial first step. Here's to your financial success!

DEFINITIONS

AGENT

A person who has been appointed to act on the behalf of another for a particular transaction,

AMENITY

Any Feature of a property that increases its value or desirability. These might include natural amenities such as location or proximity to lakes, or mountains, or man-made amenities like a swimming pool, parks or other recreation...

AMORTIZATION

The repayment of a loan through regular periodic payments over time.

AMORTIZATION SCHEDULE

The breakdown of individual payments throughout the life of an amortized loan, showing both principal and contribution and debt service (interest), fees.

AMORTIZATION TERM

The length of time in which an amortized loan is repaid. Mortgages are commonly amortized for 15/ 30 years.

ANNUAL PERCENTAGE RATE (APR)

The rate of annual interest charged on a loan.

APPRECIATION

The natural rise in property value is due to market forces.

ASSESSMENT

The function of assigning a value to a property for the purpose of levying taxes.

ASSET

An item of value, a product or service or an investment that produces cash.

BLOCKCHAIN

A decentralized, distributed and public digital ledger that is used to record transactions across many computers so that the record cannot be altered retroactively without the alteration of all subsequent blocks and the consensus of the network.

BITCOIN

It is a cryptocurrency, a virtual currency designed to act as money and a form of payment outside the control of any one person, group, or entity, thus removing the need for third-party involvement in financial transactions.

CASH-OUT REFINANCE

Refinancing a mortgage at a higher amount than the current balance in order to capture a portion of the equity in cash.

COLLATERAL

An asset that is placed at risk to secure repayment of a loan.

CONTRACT

A legally binding agreement, oral or written, between two parties.

CONVENTIONAL MORTGAGE

A traditional, real estate financing mechanism that is not backed by any Government agency (FHA, USDA, VA)

DEBT

An obligation to repay some amount owed. This may or may not be monetary.

DELINQUENCY

The state in which a borrower has failed to meet payment obligations on time.

FEE SIMPLE

A complete, unencumbered ownership right in a piece of property.

FORECLOSURE

The process whereby a lender can claim the property used by the borrower to secure a mortgage and sell the property to meet the obligation.

GRANTEE

Any person who is given ownership of a piece of property.

GRANTOR

Any person who gives away ownership of a piece of property.

HAZARD INSURANCE

Insurance covers damage to property caused by a hazard such as fire, wind, and accident.

HOME EQUALITY LINE OF CREDIT (HELOC)

A type of mortgage loan that allows the borrower to draw cash against the equity of his home.

INTESTATE

Any person who dies without executing (making) a valid last will is known as dying intestate.

LIEN

Any claim against a piece of property resulting from a debt or other obligation.

MORTGAGE

A financial arrangement wherein an individual borrows money to purchase a real property and secure the loan with the property as collateral.

POWER OF ATTORNEY

A written instrument authorizing a person, the attorney-in-fact, to act as an agent for another person to the extent indicated in the instrument.

TENANCY

The right to occupy a building or unit.

TESTATE

Having made and left a valid will.

WILL

A written document, properly witnesses, providing for the transfer of title to property owned by the deceased, called the testator.

RECOMMENDED READING

TAKING THE FIRST STEP TO FINANCIAL SECURITY- a PRIMER ON FINANCIAL LITERACY, maybe your first book that you have ever read about finance, but hopefully, it will not be your last. Once you start broadening your knowledge in the world of finance, you will learn that there is a whole new world out there where having financial knowledge reaps great rewards.

Here are six books that I highly recommend that will help in your journey:

- **Rich Dad, Poor Dad**, *by Robert Kiyosaki*

- **Cash Flow Quadrant**, *by Robert Kiyosaki*

- **Increase your Financial Literacy**, *by Robert Kiyosaki*

- **The Millionaire Next Door,** *by Thomas J Stanley, PhD*

- **The Millionaire Mind,** *by Thomas J. Stanley, PhD*

- **Think and Grow Rich,** *by Napolean Hill*

DISCLAIMER OF LIABILITY

The author nor its contributors shall be held liable for any improper or incorrect use of this information described as /or contained herein and assumes no responsibility for anyone's use of this information.

Disclaimer of warranties /accuracy of data: Although the data found using in the compilation of this book has been produced and processed from sources to be reliable, no warranty expressed or implied is made regarding is made regarding accuracy, adequacy, completeness, legality, reliability or usefulness of any information. This applies to both isolated and aggregate uses of the information.

The author has mentioned several times in the book, that it is recommended that you seek the advice of an attorney before entering into any purchase of real estate transaction.

It is further recommended that you seek out competent real estate, financial planners and loan originators who will take the time to explain and answer all your questions adequately.

Again, this book is to help educate you and better prepare you for your meeting with these professionals.

www.ingramcontent.com/pod-product-compliance
Lightning Source LLC
Chambersburg PA
CBHW071459210326
41597CB00018B/2609